GETTING YOUR POINT ACROSS IN WRITING

HOW TO WRITE ESSAYS THAT HAVE IMPACT

HERON BOOKS
K-12 CURRICULUM

Heron Books, Inc.
20950 SW Rock Creek Road
Sheridan, OR 97378

heronbooks.com

Special thanks to all the teachers and students who provided feedback instrumental to this edition.

ISBN: 0-89739-143-8

Printed in the USA

6 February 2020

At Heron Books, we think learning should be engaging and fun. It should be hands-on and it should allow students to move at their own pace.

For this purpose, we have created an accompanying learning guide to help the student progress through this book, chapter by chapter, with increasing confidence, interest and independence.

Get your free learning guide at
heronbooks.com/learningguides.

For a final exam, email
teacherresources@heronbooks.com.

We would love to hear from you!
Email us at *feedback@heronbooks.com.*

Contents

This books contains a
FREE LEARNING GUIDE

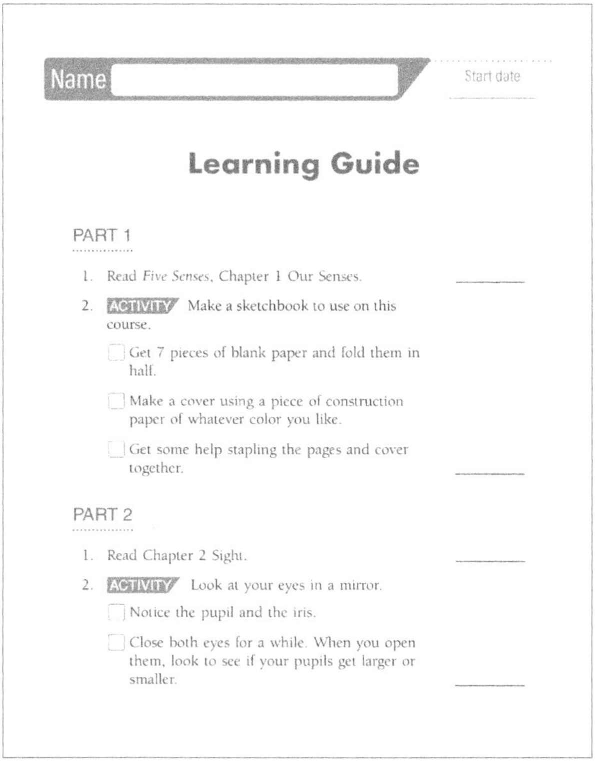

Name

Start date

Learning Guide

PART 1

1. Read *Five Senses*, Chapter 1 Our Senses.
2. ACTIVITY Make a sketchbook to use on this course.
   - [ ] Get 7 pieces of blank paper and fold them in half.
   - [ ] Make a cover using a piece of construction paper of whatever color you like.
   - [ ] Get some help stapling the pages and cover together.

PART 2

1. Read Chapter 2 Sight.
2. ACTIVITY Look at your eyes in a mirror.
   - [ ] Notice the pupil and the iris.
   - [ ] Close both eyes for a while. When you open them, look to see if your pupils get larger or smaller.

Download and print more copies at www.heronbooks.com/learningguides

Additional Resources

A **materials list** for the learning guide is at the back of this book.

For an **exam and answers**, email *teacherresources@heronbooks.com.*

GETTING YOUR POINT ACROSS IN WRITING
HOW TO WRITE ESSAYS THAT HAVE IMPACT

Name ______________________________ Date ____________

PURPOSE

Improve your ability to get a point across to others in writing.

HOW TO DO THIS COURSE: Do the steps in order. Initial and date each when done. Where there are two sign-off lines, get the step checked and initialed on the second line by another student or, if stated, by your supervisor. Have them initial the second line. All written work is turned in to the supervisor.

ESTIMATED TIME: 30 hours.

MATERIALS:
Getting Your Point Across in Writing, Heron Books

A. HAVING A POINT

1. READ: *Getting Your Point Across in Writing*, Introduction and Chapter 1 The Essay. __________

2. ACTIVITY: Think of and write down three ways you might use nonfiction writing in life. Discuss this with your supervisor. **Supervisor pass.** ____ ____

3. READ: Chapter 2 "What Is Your Point?" __________

4. ACTIVITY: Find two short, easy-to-read nonfiction books. Read enough of each book to notice what the point is. Write it down.

____

(Book title)

Point: ____

____

____

____

____

(Book title)

Point: ____

____

____

____ __________

5. READ: Chapter 3 Developing Your Ideas. __________

6. ACTIVITY: Choose a subject you know little or nothing about. Find out something about the subject by researching it for ten or fifteen minutes.

   Briefly write down what you know about the subject now.

____

____

____

____

____

____

____

Ask yourself:

- What do I think about this subject?
- What's important to me about this?
- What would I like to tell someone else about this subject?

If needed, research a bit more to answer your questions.

Continue until you know what you want to say about this subject. Note it here.

____

____

____

____

____ _________

7. READ: Chapter 4 The Subject. _________

8. ACTIVITY: You are going to start building a descriptive essay, one part at a time, as you study this book.

   Work out the subject and a point that you want to write about.

   Here are two suggestions you could use:

   - Describe your favorite place.
   - Describe how something works.

   Write down the subject and point and label your paper *Practice Essay 1*. Save this for later steps. _________

9. ACTIVITY: You are going to start building a nonfiction essay, one part at a time, as you study this book.

   Work out the subject and a point that you want to write about.

Here are some suggestions you could use:

- Write a news story about something that has happened.
- Explain how you do something. It can be how you cook something, do a hobby or sport, or build something.

Write down the subject and point and label your paper *Practice Essay 2*. Your supervisor will check that your point is what *you* want to say about the subject. Save this for later steps.

Supervisor pass. ____ ____

B. GIVING SUPPORTING DETAILS

1. READ: Chapter 5 Summarizing. ________
2. READ: Chapter 6 Details! ________
3. ACTIVITY: Choose an article from a newspaper or news magazine, online or in print. Show another student the point of the article and five details used to support it. ____ ____
4. ACTIVITY: This is the next step to building your first practice essay.

   Make a list of supporting details you could use to back up your point in *Practice Essay 1*. Save for later. ________
5. ACTIVITY: This is the next step to building your second practice essay.

   Make a list of supporting details you could use to back up your point in *Practice Essay 2*. Your supervisor will check that your details support your point adequately. Save for later. **Supervisor pass.** ____ ____

C. PLANNING THE WRITING

1. READ: Chapter 7 Outlines? Aargh! ______

2. READ: Chapter 8 The Basic Outline. ______

3. ACTIVITY: Here's the next step to writing your first practice essay.

   Write an outline for *Practice Essay 1*. You can use these questions if you wish.

   - What's the overall point?
   - Will it answer the question or assignment?
   - What are the supporting details that will help my reader understand my point?
   - How is the essay best started?
   - How is it best ended?
   - What's the best way to organize all these ideas?

   Save for later. ______

4. ACTIVITY: Here's the next step to writing your second practice essay.

   Write an outline for *Practice Essay 2*. You can use these questions if you wish.

   - What's the overall point?
   - Will it answer the question or assignment?
   - What are the supporting details that will help my reader understand my point?
   - How is the essay best started?
   - How is it best ended?
   - What's the best way to organize all these ideas?

   Your supervisor will check that your outline organizes your ideas. Save for later. **Supervisor pass.** ____ ____

D. HAVING AN INTRODUCTION, BODY AND CONCLUSION

1. READ: Chapter 9 The Intro or "Lead." __________

2. ACTIVITY: Choose three history, biography, or nonfiction books.

   Read the first page or two of each one. Notice if the beginning interests you enough to keep reading the book.

   Work out why the intro was or wasn't interesting to you.

   Decide which intro was the most interesting. __________

3. READ: Chapter 10 The Body or "Story." __________

4. ACTIVITY: Read three short newspaper or magazine articles, online or in print. Pay attention to the body of the articles.

   What did you notice?

   Which was most effective in getting its point across to you?

   Did it follow any of the tips in chapter 10 or was it written differently?

   Choose the body that best communicated the message of the article. What did you like about it? __________

5. READ: Chapter 11 The Conclusion or "Close." __________

6. ACTIVITY: Using the same articles from the previous activity, read the concluding paragraphs.

   Do they conclude or close the articles well?

   Choose the conclusion you feel ended its article best. What did you like about it? __________

7. ACTIVITY: Here's the next step to writing your first practice essay.

   Using the point, supporting details and outline you prepared for *Practice Essay 1*, write your full essay with an introduction, body and conclusion. Save it for later. ________

8. ACTIVITY: This is the next step to writing your second practice essay.

   Using the point, supporting details and outline you prepared for *Practice Essay 2,* write your full essay with an introduction, body and conclusion. This is the first draft. Your supervisor will check that the intro, body, and conclusion serve their purposes. Save it for later. **Supervisor pass.** ____ ____

9. READ: Chapter 12 Connecting Ideas. ________

10. ACTIVITY: Get an easy-to-read nonfiction book. Read a few pages and notice if there are transition words or phrases. For each transition, tell someone how these words or phrases connect one idea to the next. ____ ____

11. ACTIVITY: This is the next step to writing your first practice essay.

    Read your *Practice Essay 1* and locate any sentences or paragraphs that don't seem to connect very well or jump too quickly from one idea to the next. Improve the flow from one idea to the next using transition words or phrases. Save your essay for later. ________

12. ACTIVITY: Here's the next step to writing your second practice essay.

    Read your *Practice Essay 2* and locate any sentences or paragraphs that don't seem to connect very well or jump too quickly from one idea to the next. Improve the flow from one idea to the next using transition words, phrases, or sentences. Your supervisor will check that your sentences and paragraphs flow smoothly from one idea to the next. Save your essay for later. **Supervisor pass.** ____ ____

E. WRITING DIFFERENT TYPES OF ESSAYS

1. READ: Chapter 13 "But *How* Do I Write an Essay?" ________

2. READ: Chapter 14 The Narrative Essay. ________

3. ACTIVITY: Choose a subject and a point for a narrative essay. Decide whether you will tell the story from your viewpoint or someone else's.

   Here are some suggestions:

   - write about a time you (or they) enjoyed doing something
   - write a narrative of a funny, but true story
   - write a play-by-play narrative of a game

   Write a narrative essay about anything you choose. Make sure you get your point across. ____ ____

4. READ: Chapter 15 The Descriptive Essay. ________

5. ACTIVITY: Write a detailed description of a well-known character in a book or movie without stating that person's name. Give it to someone to read and ask them to guess the name of the character you are writing about.

   If your reader can't guess who the character is, read your writing and add or delete details to make your description clearer. Ask someone to read it now and guess the name of the character you are writing about. ____ ____

6. READ: Chapter 16 The Expository Essay. ________

7.ACTIVITY: In writing, explain how something works. Some suggestions you could use are:

- How a bicycle works or how to change a bike tire
- How a computer works or how any machine works
- What causes the seasons

Your supervisor will check that your explanation is logical and easy to understand.

Supervisor pass. ____ ____

8. READ: Chapter 17 The Persuasive Essay. ________

9. READ: Chapter 18 Outside the Box. ________

10. ACTIVITY: Choose a viewpoint or opinion you have and write a persuasive essay on it.

    When you are satisfied with it, have someone else read it. Then ask them if your essay persuaded them to agree with your viewpoint.

    If they were not persuaded or convinced, find out why and read your essay to see what you could add or delete to make it more persuasive.

    Then ask the same person to read it again and tell you if the writing persuaded them. ____ ____

F. REVISING AND PROOFREADING

1. READ: Chapter 19 Getting It Right. ________

2. READ: Chapter 20 Feedback. ________

3. ACTIVITY: This is the next step to writing your first practice essay.

    a) Read your *Practice Essay 1* and mark any points you can improve. Then revise the paper and make a new draft. ____

b) Continue to revise and rewrite your essay until you are satisfied it effectively gets your point across. ___

c) Ask someone else to read it and give you feedback. Make further revisions if needed. ___

d) Correct any errors in spelling, punctuation, and so on. ___

e) Turn in your final essay.

Supervisor pass. ___ ___

4. ACTIVITY: Here's the next step to writing your second practice essay.

   a) Read your *Practice Essay* 2 and mark any points you can improve. Then revise the paper accordingly and make a new draft. ___

   b) Continue to revise and rewrite your essay until you are satisfied it effectively gets your point across. ___

   c) Ask someone else to read it and give you feedback. Make further revisions if needed. ___

   d) Correct any errors in spelling, punctuation, and so on. ___

   e) Turn in your final essay.

   Supervisor pass. ___ ___

G. AVOIDING PLAGIARISM

1. READ: Chapter 21 "Whose Ideas Are These?" ___ ___

2. ACTIVITY: Write a short essay that explains and gives examples when you would need to note where you got words or ideas that weren't yours. Also explain how you could show that, and why you would show it. ___ ___

H. FINAL ACTIVITIES

1. READ: Chapter 22 Putting It All Together. ________

2. (Optional) READ: Chapter 23 Final Tips (for aspiring professionals). ________

3. ACTIVITY: Write anything you wish. This is some writing you can do without anyone else correcting it. You can write nonfiction or fiction. Just write several paragraphs as clearly as you can about anything that interests you. ________

4. ACTIVITY: Decide on a subject and a point to write about in a persuasive essay. Keep in mind the specific type of person or group you want to persuade with your essay. Then using what you learned in this book and the points in "Putting It All Together," revise and rewrite it until you are satisfied it gets your point across and it has no errors. ____ ____

5. ACTIVITY: Choose a new subject to write a longer essay. Using what you learned in this book and the points in "Putting It All Together," make sure your writing clearly gets your point across and has no errors.

   Supervisor pass. ____ ____

I have completed the steps of this course. I understand what I studied and can use it.

Student ______________________ Date ______________

The student has completed the steps of this course and knows and can apply what was studied.

Academic supervisor ____________________ Date ________________

The student has passed the exam for this course.

Examiner ______________________________ Date ________________

FOR FACULTY

NOTE

This course assumes a student has the knowledge and abilities obtained from *Writing Paragraphs* and *Working with Essays* (able to write sentences and paragraphs well, capitalization and punctuation).

MATERIALS NEEDED FOR THIS COURSE

Access to a newspaper or news magazine, and several history, biography or nonfiction books.

ADDITIONAL RESOURCES

Exam and answers

25 January 2020

Introduction

A few years ago, a dairy farmer in Oregon was told she could not legally advertise the raw milk from her grass-fed cows. She could sell it, but she couldn't advertise it! Suddenly, she found herself needing to write articles, letters, and even speeches for public hearings. After months of work, she got the law changed.

She was fortunate. She could write. More to the point: she could write *well.*

Unfortunately, many young people today are completing high school, even college, without the ability to write well. The ability to read and write is one thing. The ability to read and write *well* is another.

An informal survey of leaders in business, science, humanities and the arts resulted in a list of the top four qualities most desired in employees and associates:

- honesty and integrity
- the ability to work well with others
- initiative
- the ability to write well

The first three may not be surprising, but why *the ability to write well*?

As in the case of the dairy farmer who needed to support her family and protect her way of life, the answer lies in the importance of ideas and their successful distribution.

Through reports, proposals, blogs, webpages, social media, magazines or books,

strong writing allows important ideas to be shared.

Whether you struggle with writing or love it, whether you are a student wanting to write better essays or just someone wanting to improve your writing, this book was written to give you simple tools for getting your point across in writing.

Are you ready?

The Essay

In school, you may often be asked to "write an essay on _________." But what exactly does that mean?

The simplest definition of **essay** is this:

a short piece of writing on some subject,
usually presenting the writer's personal views.

This definition is often applied to students, but it also applies to professionals in many fields. When someone is writing to make some point, to communicate what they see, what they think, what *they* have to say about some topic, it's an essay.

The basics of essay writing, learned well, can then be applied to almost all types of nonfiction writing:

Writing a proposal

Writing about research

Writing about why a certain thing should be done

Writing a strategy or plan for achieving something

Writing an analysis or explanation of some situation

That's a wide range of writing, but the basics of essay writing apply to all of them. If you can't write a good essay, you won't be able to do the kind of writing you will need in the real world of pursuing your goals and dreams.

If you can write a good essay, you can write. And

***the key to writing a good essay is
having a point and getting it across.***

"What Is Your Point?"

The worst thing that can happen to you when you try to communicate something in writing is to have your reader respond:

"Okay, so what is your point?"

If you have ever had this happen, you know the feeling—especially if you worked hard on trying to get some point across.

So, let's start by making very sure we know what we are talking about when we talk about this word *point.*

point

The main message or opinion you want to communicate.
What you want to say.

But let's look a little more closely at this word.

Point can also mean:

The reason or purpose for something.
Why something exists or why something is done.

If someone reads an essay or other piece of nonfiction writing you've done and says, "What is your point?" they aren't just saying, "What is your main message?" They are also saying, "Why did you write this? What purpose are you trying to achieve?"

The simplest advice on essay writing is this:

Have a clear purpose and know what you want to say.

Don't ever write an essay if you don't have anything to say.

That also means don't ever write an essay that just repeats what someone else said. What's the point? (There's that word again.) They've already said it.

Sometimes, however, you will be asked to write an essay and you'll realize you're not sure what exactly you want to say about the topic.

Good! That's the first place to start and the subject of the next chapter.

Developing Your Ideas

Again, the simplest advice on good essay writing is *have a clear purpose and know what you want to say.*

What do you do if that doesn't come easily? You have two choices:

1. Write a pointless essay that's of no interest to you or anyone else.
2. Develop your ideas until you are clear on what point you want to make.

But what does that mean exactly?

What is meant here by **develop your ideas** is

to study, learn, find out more;
to work the topic around until something about it
grabs you, until something "clicks."

Ask yourself questions like this:

- What do *I* really think about this?
- What's important to *me* about this topic?
- What are *my* thoughts on this, even if I'm not sure they're worth sharing?

This last point can be a hidden barrier to good writing: the person thinks their own ideas aren't interesting enough, good enough or important enough to share.

This sort of thinking is probably the biggest reason for every failure that ever happened in the history of the world! Someone thought their ideas weren't interesting enough, good enough or important enough to communicate.

It's not a very good excuse.

You have your ideas. Don't be afraid to share them. The worst that can happen is someone will disagree with you. Great! Maybe you'll end up learning something. Maybe you'll succeed in getting the other person to reexamine their own ideas. Maybe both of these things will happen. Whatever happens, your communication can be the first step toward changing the way things are.

Almost every teacher will tell you their favorite students are the ones who are not afraid to say what they think, *if they say it well.* Teachers love learning from students.

And the best leaders in the world totally depend on hearing and learning from the people they are trying to lead. Their ability to listen and learn is an important part of how they got where they are.

So, if you need to write an essay (or a proposal, an analysis, or anything else), and you aren't really sure what you want to say, don't start writing.

Develop your ideas!

Study more, look at the topic more deeply or more closely, compare it to what you know and what you believe.

Eventually, you will have something to say.
You will have a point to make.

The Subject

So, you've developed your ideas and you know what point you want to make.

Great. Now you know what the subject of your essay is. Right?

Well, no, not exactly. This confusion of terms not only causes problems for essay writers, it often results in the unwanted response: "So what is your point?"

Let's clear this up right now.

The **subject** of an essay is

the general area you are writing about.

The **point** of an essay is

your own message or opinion about the subject,
what *you* think and what *you* want to say about the subject.

Here's an example:

> After reading a book about a family trying to survive a war, you might be asked to write an essay on the subject of courage.
>
> For you, the mother showed the most courage because she risked her own life to protect and care for her children. When you read the book, or when you thought about the essay assignment, that's the idea that grabbed you, the idea that "clicked": *This woman repeatedly risked her own life to protect and care for her children.*

That's the *point* you want to make on the *subject* of courage as it relates to this book.

Taking it a step further, there might be a deeper point you want to make: *I wonder if I would ever have the kind of courage this woman showed. It inspired me, but it also frightened me.*

Now that would be an interesting essay to read!

Here's another example:

> You are writing an article for a school website about a trip with fellow students to an athletic shoe factory.
>
> The subject is the field trip to the factory. But you could have many different points you want to make about the trip.
>
> - What the trip got you thinking about in terms of your own career.
> - Why the trip was so rewarding to so many students.
> - How the technology of athletic shoe construction and design is changing all the time.
> - What you learned about organization, leadership or marketing.
> - Why the trip was unfortunately a waste of time and how it could have been planned better. (It probably wouldn't get posted on the website, but if that's all you honestly have to say, the trip shouldn't be promoted on the website! And your essay could become a useful proposal to those responsible for planning future trips like this one.)

When students aren't taught to make their own point in writing essays, they begin to think that there's only one "right answer" to everything. That's very rarely true.

Know your subject,
develop your own ideas,
then make your point.

Otherwise, you might end up with the response, "So what is your point?"

Summarizing

Another common mistake in essays is just summarizing things you've learned.

To **summarize** is to

tell the main facts or ideas about something
in a short amount of space or time.

We often need to summarize things. For example, when you're telling someone about a soccer game you played that afternoon, you won't describe every play. You'll talk about the main things that happened that made the game successful or unsuccessful.

In the example of the essay on courage from the previous chapter, you might summarize a portion of the woman's life as part of your essay. That's fine.

But there are two problems with summaries in essay writing:

1. If you end up just summarizing, you can forget to make *your* point.

2. Summaries are usually boring. Details are usually interesting.

The first problem is similar to the confusion discussed in the previous chapter. You can write about the subject without making any point. You can also fall into summarizing and forget that an essay is for sharing your own views on the topic.

Dealing with the second problem is the subject of the next chapter—details!

Meanwhile,

if you find you're doing a lot of summarizing,
you're probably on the wrong track.

Details!

Details are

small, specific facts or pieces of information;
the things you see when you look closely.

Using details can take something from boring to interesting.

No details:

> We got to visit a professional basketball stadium. I couldn't believe how big it was. It was impressive.

With details:

> We got to visit a professional basketball stadium. We were each given a tennis ball and asked if we could hit the ceiling with it. Fernando, who has a strong arm, could barely reach the scoreboard, which hangs way down from the ceiling. When I watch basketball on tv, the stadiums look small. But that's probably because it's on tv and because professional basketball players are all between 6 and 7 feet tall! I counted over 250 seats in one small section. That's way more people than filled our home gym last night. I just couldn't believe how huge the place was.

You might think the main difference is that the second paragraph is just longer. That's true. It is longer. But the main difference is that it provides details: tennis balls, scoreboards, ceilings, tv, 7-foot-tall men, 250 seats, home gym, last night, and so on. Those things are all details.

This leads right into the topic of *supporting details.*

When something *supports* something else, it
holds it up, keeping it from falling apart or falling down.

It also means

help prove that something is correct or true.

If you think of the Statue of Liberty, you may be able to picture in your mind the large pedestal and base that support it. (If not, you can look it up.) The statue is about 150 feet (45 meters) tall. The base and pedestal together are about 150 feet tall. That's a lot of support to keep the statue from falling down!

If someone is trying to convince you to do something, you might need enough details so that you will agree that what they're telling you is a good idea. It needs enough support to keep the main idea from collapsing.

In your essay writing (or similar kinds of writing), **supporting details** are

specifics or examples that support and prove your point;
information that helps the reader *see* what you are trying to say.

When you have a point to make, you want to give enough supporting details so the reader can clearly see why your point makes sense.

Let's say you went to see a new movie and didn't like it. Here are three versions of describing it to someone.

1. It's boring. Don't see it.

2. Oh, you know, boy meets girl, they hate each other, then they "shockingly" fall in love. Same old story. Boring.

3. Well, it's about a woman who hires a deadbeat writer to work for her outdoor adventure magazine. For most of the movie, he drives her crazy by being stupid and irresponsible, like turning in the wrong story right on the deadline and then being unreachable for two days. In the end, they "shockingly" fall in love. Bad writing, average acting, stupid plot. No awards coming here!

Each of these descriptions has their use. For some situations, the first one is fine. It's simple and to the point! The second one, though quite short, is fairly informative and would work for some situations. The third one, however, provides a bit more detail: deadbeat writer, outdoor adventure magazine, stupid and irresponsible guy, stories, deadlines, and at least a comment on the writing, acting and plot.

The third example provides enough supporting details to really make the point. The first two make a point, but with little or no supporting details. If you were planning on seeing the movie, either of the first two examples might not convince you not to go.

Of course, with the supporting details of the third example, you might decide that's the kind of movie you want to see, even though your friend clearly did not like it.

One way to think of this, as it applies to essay writing, is this:

Your point is the goal you arrived at, the conclusion you made, your main message. But how did you get there? What path of details led you to that conclusion? A good writer will take readers down that same path so they arrive at the same place.

In other words, they get the point of the essay!

Like this:

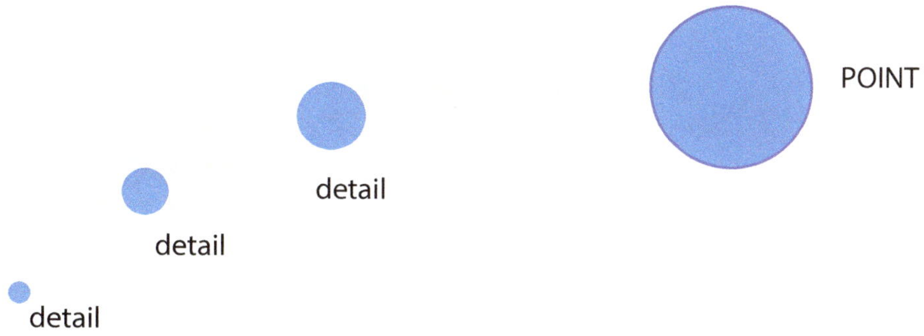

Without good supporting details,
the best points in the world often fall short.

Outlines? Aargh!

If you've ever been asked to write an outline before writing a paper, you may feel about outlines like you feel about going to the dentist.

If so, set those feelings aside.

Outlines are actually useful—and easy!

If you're someone who can write great essay after great essay without ever writing an outline, wonderful. Hopefully, nobody will ever ask to see your outline. If the essays are well-written and effective, nobody should care about the outline.

But most of us need to be organized to get much done. And that's all an outline is for: planning the path of ideas that will get your overall point across.

Most simply, an **outline** is

the main points of a plan or a piece of writing,
minus the details.

In any profession involving creative or constructive work, planning is a key part of success. You can probably think of your own examples, but here are a couple:

Portrait artists don't start with the details. They get the overall shapes worked out on the canvas to ensure the overall dimensions are right. They get basic color themes worked out so they know which layers of color will go down first. Gradually, they build a portrait, step by step, ending with the finer details that make the portrait jump off the canvas, capturing the personality of their subject for the viewer.

High-level athletic team coaches often prepare their teams for each specific opponent. They know what the other team's strengths and weaknesses are. They know what their own players are capable of, what their own team's strengths and weaknesses are. They plan the type of defense they will play and the type of offense they will play. They work out a strategy, communicate it to the players, and then go over details, such as who will cover whom, which plays to use in certain situations, and so on.

An outline is where you come up with a plan. It's like the developing sketch of the portrait painter or the overall strategy developed by the coach.

For a short essay, a quick mental sketch is often enough. But to write a longer essay that has impact, you will usually need to start with some kind of outline. Putting together an outline might involve asking yourself questions like these:

- What's the overall point?
- Will it answer the question or assignment?
- What are the supporting details that will help me get my reader to arrive there?
- How is the essay best started?
- How is it best ended?
- What's the best way to organize all these ideas?

In addition to helping ensure you effectively get your point across, there's another great reason for having an outline before you start:

Good outlines save you lots of wasted time!

Unless you are the kind of person who can think several moves ahead in a game of chess, writing a long essay without any outline will rarely work.[1] After writing, you will realize you didn't make the point clearly, the supporting details weren't in an order that made sense, you wrote a great essay but failed to actually answer the question, or something

1 Even if you are on your way to being a chess master, you may first need to get as good at writing as you are at chess before you're able to visualize a winning outline for a long essay!

else went wrong. You'll end up having to re-do all or major portions of your work. A good outline can help save you from at least some of that.

But again, realize that writing an outline isn't hard—it's easy.

An outline is just a basic plan. It's like pulling out the map before taking off on a long hike. With no plan or path, you're probably going to get lost.

There's also the subject of originality and differences between essays. If you only had to write the same essay over and over, you wouldn't need an outline. You would just do the same thing you did before.

Construction contractors (those in charge of all the different crews involved in building a house or other building) have to have a different plan for every project. If every building or house they make is exactly the same, one plan works every time. But if they want a unique building, they need a unique plan for each one.

If you want a unique essay,
you need a unique outline.

Otherwise, every essay you write will sound just like the one you wrote before.

If the essay is very short, writing an outline that you don't really need is silly. But not writing an outline when you actually need one is sillier. If you're walking up the hill behind your house, you don't need a plan. If you want to climb Mt. Kilimanjaro or Mt. Everest, you better have a very good, very detailed plan!

Fortunately, essay writing isn't a life-or-death activity. You can learn from your mistakes and live to try again!

Once you've written a few outlines and seen how they can help you, you'll discover how easy and useful they can be.

And one more thing:

Plans can change. So can outlines.

The contractor may discover the plans looked great on paper, but the storage closet the home buyer wanted under the stairs doesn't fit there. The coach may discover in the middle of the game that the strategy backfired and it's time to go to Plan B, quick!

If your outline isn't working, there's no rule that says you can't change it. In fact, it's normal for outlines to change as a writer is developing a piece of writing.

The Basic Outline

As discussed in the previous chapter, if you want a unique piece of writing, you'll want an outline that works for that particular piece of writing.

Still, there is a basic outline that you will never write but you should understand. And this is something you may have heard before and you may hear again:

intro, body, conclusion

Let's talk about what this actually means.

An **intro**, or introduction, is

how something starts,
particularly a speech or piece of writing.

The problem with this word is that past textbooks and teachers often said that an introduction should summarize the main points you intend to cover in the essay. This introduces the problem that comes with summarizing, as discussed in an earlier chapter: summaries lack details and are often boring. Textbooks, particularly older ones, often give examples of introductions based on this summary idea; they are not examples of good writing. Good writers don't write introductions that are summaries.

Today, professional writers for magazines or online publications talk about the *lead* instead of the *intro.* That's *lead* (leed), like the verb "to lead."

When talking about writing, the **lead** is

the first paragraph or two of a piece of writing,
designed to get the reader's attention and pull (or lead) them in.

A writer *might* decide to lead the reader in by giving a summary of where the essay (or other piece of writing) is going. But if it doesn't do a good job of leading them in, it's probably not a good way to start the essay.

Have you ever watched a movie preview and decided there was now no point in seeing the movie because the preview basically told the whole story? That's very much like what students have been taught about introductions.

Here's an example:

> In this essay, I'm going to discuss my reasons for joining my school choir. I'm going to talk about the ways it helped me make friends, learn more about music, improve my social skills and give me something to do at school that I truly enjoy.

There's no point in reading the essay—you already know what it's going to say!

So, when you think of writing your *intro*, think like a professional writer and try to write a *lead* that will interest the reader and make them want to continue.

When talking about an essay, **body** is a fancy word for

the main part of the essay itself.

That's all there is to it.

Let's compare an essay to taking a hike. When you take a hike, you start somewhere and end somewhere. What's in between the start and the end? The hike!

What's the *body* of an essay? It's the essay—minus whatever you did to get the reader started and whatever you do to wrap the essay up. It's the main part of the essay.

In writing, or anything else, the **conclusion** is

the end, the wrap-up;
the final answer, decision or overall point.

Unfortunately, many students have been given a troublesome definition for this word as well. They've been taught that a conclusion is a summary of the main points of an essay. There's that word again: summary.

If you write a conclusion that summarizes, you will end up with something like this:

> In this essay, I've explained why I am so glad I joined the school choir. I showed how it helped me make friends, learn more about music, improve my social skills, and it gave me something to do at school that I truly enjoy. I'm so glad I joined the choir.

The end result of these explanations for *intro* and *conclusion* is that many students have gotten the idea they should do this:

> Intro: Summarize the main point and the main ideas
>
> Body: Write about the main point and the main ideas.
>
> Conclusion: Summarize the main point and the main ideas.

This is *not* how to write a good essay or paper.

Maybe you have never written or seen this kind of essay. It's still something to watch out for because even though many teachers and textbooks don't teach these things anymore, some teachers will still expect you to write essays with these wrong definitions of *intro* and *conclusion.*

What does make sense is this:

Get your reader interested in going somewhere,
show them some things that are interesting or useful along the way,
then end the adventure smoothly.

When we talk about *the basic outline,* that's what it *should* mean.

And that's what a good essay will do.

The Intro or "Lead"

So, you've developed your ideas and know what overall *point* you want to make.

You've worked out an outline, a path for taking your reader where you want to take them. You know what you want to say and have a good sketch for the order of ideas that will get your point across.

It's time to start actually writing. It's time to write your intro or "lead."

You may have some idea of how you want to start, or you may not. Either way, what is staring back at you is a blank piece of paper or an empty document on your screen.

Let's start tackling this by reviewing the definition we're using for **lead**:

the first paragraph or two of a piece of writing,
designed to get the reader's attention and pull (or lead) them in.

A useful suggestion in creating your intro or lead is this: don't spend too much time trying to get it perfect the first time. Get something written that gets you started and then carry on with writing the rest of the essay (or article, proposal, research paper, or whatever it is). Once you have a first draft of your essay and you feel like you're getting your point across, you can always come back and improve your introduction.

This is particularly useful advice, especially when combined with this fact:

Many professional writers will tell you that a great lead is often the hardest part of writing a really strong essay.

So even though the intro comes first, it might be the last thing you put extra time into getting right!

Let's talk about some ideas on how to interest your reader. These are just tips. You can really start an essay any way you want.

Each tip will be followed by a short example or two. Leads can be longer, of course.

1. **Don't summarize. Use details.**

Chapters 5 and 6 talk about summaries (boring) and details (interesting). This applies to the essay overall, but it especially applies to good leads.

> Staring for minutes at a blank screen, fingers on the keyboard, head full of information on the Civil War? It must be time to write another essay and once again you have no idea where to start!

Notice the details: blank screen, fingers, keyboard, head. This could have been the lead to this chapter. The reader can tell where it's going, and the details make it more interesting than just summarizing what is going to be said about how to start an essay.

2. **Create a picture or scene. Put the reader there.**

Pick the most meaningful scene that ties in to your point, then describe that scene in detail.

Here's an example:

> Megan holds her grandmother's head gently in her lap. The rain taps on the roof the same as it has for days. She wonders, again, "How can I ask her about Mother without upsetting her? What if I never have the courage to find out what happened that summer before I was born?"

This creates a scene and uses details to do so. It leads the reader in. Though this sounds like the beginning of a fiction story, this can be recreating a scene from a literature book where you've been asked to talk about something you learned or that was meaningful.

A lead like this can be used for almost any type of essay. It's a very common type of lead for magazine articles.

3. Start with one or more strong facts.

Facts are details. They can be a good way to quickly interest the reader.

> Have you ever wondered how people who can't read and write fill out medical forms? Over $200 billion is wasted every year because thirty-six million American adults are illiterate. Imagine how much more is wasted in other areas. Isn't there something we can do about this huge problem?

Again, the purpose of the intro, or lead, is to draw the reader in while giving some idea where you are going.

4. Make it personal.

Usually an essay is for communicating what *you* think, what *you* have to say, *your* thoughts, opinions or conclusions. Therefore, starting off with something about yourself, your experience, your ideas or an event in your life can work well.

> Kathy, Jens, Chloe and I worked for three hours at the food bank last week. When we finished, we were told our work would help feed over fifty people for a month. I never thought I could make that much of a difference in other people's lives with a few hours of my time.

We don't yet know if the essay is going to be about the food bank, about how much difference one person can make in the lives of others, or about what the person has learned from community service activities. But the personal intro makes it more realistic and more interesting.

5. Present the reader with a question or problem.

Here's a simple example:

> Why should teens be asked to read books about people from other parts of the world? Is this really going to help them in college or in their careers?

Whatever you write for your intro or lead, the key is to

draw the reader in and
give them some idea what the essay is about.

The Body or "Story"

We defined **body** in chapter 8 this way:

the main part of the essay itself.

Here are some tips that provide more information on writing the body of an essay:

1. Keep to the path. Maintain a logical flow.

Again, an essay can be thought of like a hike. When you follow a path, you go from one point to the next, then the next, then the next. You don't suddenly teleport[2] from the top of a hill to a valley a mile away. You walk down the hill, cross the creek and head toward the valley. It's the same with an essay. You move from one point to the next, then the next, then the next. It makes sense as it moves along.

This is often described as keeping a *logical flow* in your writing. What you don't want to happen is to have your reader suddenly go, "Huh? How did we get here?" You want them to move along smoothly, following your path of logic or reasoning.

This is partly where *story* comes in. For our purposes here, a **story** is

the telling or description of something that happened, usually as a sequence of actions.

2 Teleport: To move (people or objects) across distances instantly, something only achieved in science fiction, so far.

Thinking of the body of the essay as a story can help you with the idea of logical flow.

2. Let your reasons, examples or arguments build up.

When you are trying to convince someone of something, the reasons you give are sometimes called **arguments**. Your outline for this kind of writing will consist mainly of your different reasons or arguments.

As you go along, it is sometimes smart to save your best reasons, arguments or examples for last. If you are doing a good job of convincing someone of your main point through your examples or reasons, by the time they get to your best ones, they will already be pretty well convinced. The last one just makes sure!

3. Don't avoid counter-arguments; use them.

A **counter-argument** is something that goes against what you are trying to say.

If the point of an essay is "Thirteen-year-olds can read and enjoy Shakespeare," a counter-argument might be "students shouldn't have to read books with lots of unfamiliar words." It's an argument that goes counter to (directly against) the point.

When you are trying to make a point, particularly if you are writing a proposal or trying to convince someone of something, you might think it's a bad idea to introduce counter-arguments. After all, why would you want to tell your reader reasons they *shouldn't* agree with you?

Well, it's usually best to bring up good counter-arguments yourself. Here's why.

Imagine someone is trying to convince you to go on a bike ride with them because it will be fun. (That's their main *argument*: it will be fun.) Unfortunately, it's raining. (That would be a *counter-argument*: it's raining.) If they don't say anything about the rain, you will think they don't know or just don't care that it's raining. As soon as they start talking about going on a bike ride, you might just ignore them. On the other hand, if they know the rain will stop you from going, they can say right away that they know it's raining (counter-argument), but they have a solution or reasons why the rain won't be a problem or isn't as important as their main argument.

Think like the reader. What will the reader think you are avoiding or not thinking of? By bringing up counter-arguments early, you can then address them by showing why your arguments, reasons or examples are more important.

4. Consider taking the reader down the path you followed.

When you write an essay, you are normally sharing your opinion or viewpoint on a particular subject. You might be answering a particular question or set of questions. You might be trying to convince the reader of something you believe. Or you might simply be sharing something you learned.

This is another place where the idea of *story* comes in.

Again, let's consider an essay like a hike.

If you took a hike and ended up at a beautiful waterfall with a swimming hole at the bottom, you might want to share the experience with someone else. You have two options:

1) You can blindfold them, take them there, then show it to them; or

2) You can take them with you and show them not only the beautiful destination but how you got there.

In an essay, you normally want to do the second one: take the reader down the path you followed. Again, think of it like a story. It's the story of your adventure to arriving at your opinion or conclusion—your *point.*

If your essay doesn't have a lot of arguments and counter-arguments and you're wondering what the body of the essay should consist of, think of it like a story. What story is worth telling that will lead to your overall message? If there is one, and it's worth telling, then tell it!

5. Try telling someone your essay before outlining it.

The last tip in this chapter is this: If you are having a hard time figuring out exactly how to make your point, and you can't seem to come up with an outline, try just telling someone what you want to say.

For most of us, talking is much easier than writing because we talk more than we write. By sitting down and just telling someone what you think you want to say, you might find the outline starting to take shape. Listen to what you are saying and make some notes of your main ideas.

It just might get you rolling!

The Conclusion or "Close"

The last part of an essay is the conclusion.

We defined an essay's **conclusion** as

> the end, the wrap-up;
> the final answer, decision or overall point.

This is where you achieve your final destination, the end of the hike.

If you built up your arguments well, it should now be easy to tell your reader,

> Therefore, the obvious answer (or decision or conclusion) is ________.

> The solution to this problem is clearly ________.

Or simply conclude with your overall point.

You can also call this wrap-up the *closing* or *close* (pronounced kloze), which is a term usually used for speeches but works for essays as well. **Close** is defined this way:

> the end or conclusion of a performance;
> the final part of a communication.

Like your intro (or lead), your conclusion (or close) should be strong. You want to make the reader feel like everything has been said and the overall message is clear.

In a short essay, it might be just one sentence. In a longer essay, it might be a paragraph or two.

Here are some tips on writing essay conclusions:

1. **Invite, encourage, or demand action.**

Depending on the essay, you might be trying to get the reader to do something. If it's a proposal, you are suggesting a solution to a problem, situation or opportunity.

> Based on all this information, we should act soon on getting a new 3D printer for the science lab, especially with the dependable Aaxon Model 4 on sale for the next week only.

If it's a topic you feel strongly about and you have been effective in stirring the emotions of your reader, what you probably want is for the reader to *act.*

> Reverend Dr. Martin Luther King has shown us the way. You and I must follow his lead every day and *do our part* in treating every human being with respect. Can you, will you, help me make a difference?

Encouraging action can be a great way to end many types of nonfiction writing.

2. **Come back to your introduction and "close the circle."**

An essay, or any longer communication, can be thought of like a circle. If you do it well, it comes back around to the place it started without leaving any holes or gaps in the circle (it kept a logical flow).

If you start off with your overall message or point as part of your intro, it often makes sense to come back around and repeat that same point at the end, even if you decide to say it a little bit differently.

Here's an example of closing the circle on an essay which started with the message "Happiness is sometimes found in places you never expect to find it."

> By the last day of summer, Gabrielle had spent almost a year helping her brother relearn how to walk. Every day had been a challenge and there had been many arguments and many tears. But on that day, she noticed that she had forgotten all about her own teenage problems. Instead she realized how much she loved her brother and how proud she was to have helped him.

3. Connect the close to the lead.

This is similar to #2, but not the same. Here you are completing the circle by just connecting your closing sentence or paragraph back to something you led the essay with, such as a personal anecdote or a specific scene.

Let's use the example lead of the scene where Megan was holding her grandmother's head in her lap, wondering if she'd ever have the courage to ask something about her mother. Here's an example close for that imaginary essay:

> In the end, her grandmother said, "Meg, you are a brave young woman. Your mother would be very proud of you. And no matter what happens in life, don't ever be afraid of secrets." I hope I can always be as courageous as Megan was.

In this short paragraph, the writer connects the close to the lead and also makes her final point in the last sentence. If the lead pulled the reader in, and if the body was well organized and went logically forward, step by step, this close will help ensure the writer's point got across.

4. Leave the reader with something to think about.

Sometimes the best nonfiction writing doesn't actually answer the question directly. It leaves readers to answer the question themselves.

Should we really invest trillions and trillions of dollars trying to create places on Mars where humans can live when we have millions of people struggling to live on Earth?

Do you believe every human being is capable of something truly great?

Am I really responsible for everything that happens around me? Are you?

In each of these examples, your essay probably showed where you stand and what you think. But leaving the reader with a question is a way to involve them personally in your thinking or overall point.

This kind of closing can be trickier to do well, but try it out now and then and see if it helps you get your point across more effectively.

No matter how you close an essay, the important thing is to

make the reader feel like they've completed the trip smoothly.

Connecting Ideas

Chapter 10 talked about keeping to the path or maintaining a logical flow with your ideas. Good outlining helps this. But even if the essay isn't that long and doesn't require an outline, you want the reader to move smoothly from one idea to the next.

Learning to write well includes learning how to connect ideas together as you go.

Mostly, you will find that this comes naturally. But here's a way it's described that can help you understand it better.

Transition means

moving or changing from one thing or condition
to a different one.

Transition words or phrases are

words or groups of words
that help connect sentences or paragraphs together.

Sometimes they are just called *transitions.*

Here's an example of a transition phrase that helps connect two sentences:

> Tim learned to read music at a young age. <u>As a result</u>, by his teens he could easily look over a piece of music and get an idea what it would sound like.

Now, you might think it makes perfect sense without that phrase. Let's try it:

> Tim learned to read music at a young age. By his teens he could easily look over a piece of music and get an idea what it would sound like.

That doesn't sound bad, does it? It depends on which one you prefer and how it fits in with the rest of the essay.

Here's another example of a transition between two sentences:

> If your point is too broad, you may have trouble convincing a reader that your viewpoint makes sense. If you find this in your essay, make your point more focused so you can support it well with details.

The underlined group of words helps connect the two ideas. Again, let's try removing that phrase and see how it sounds:

> If your point is too broad, you may have trouble convincing a reader that your viewpoint makes sense. Make your point more focused so you can support it well with details.

That one doesn't work so well. You need some kind of transition, even a simple one like the word *therefore.* Let's try that:

> If your point is too broad, you may have trouble convincing a reader that your viewpoint makes sense. Therefore, make your point more focused so you can support it well with details.

The word *therefore* successfully connects the two ideas.

Words and phrases commonly used to connect sentences include these:

thus	though	finally
so	otherwise	again
therefore	for example	besides
as a result	for instance	similarly
because of this	specifically	in the same way
even though	then	in this way
however	next	for this reason

Again, you will generally find the use of these comes naturally. In fact, you could make the mistake of using them too much, which would be distracting and would sound strange.

Transitioning from one paragraph to another is similar. Here's an example of a sentence that starts a paragraph in a way that connects it to what was being talked about before:

> Even though the government of Nepal has not been able to stop all illegal hunting of tigers, they have made great progress in recent years.

The previous paragraph, though not shown here, was obviously talking about the trouble the Nepalese government had controlling illegal tiger hunting. The underlined group of words helps connect the previous topic to the new topic about to be discussed—the great progress in recent years.

Knowing about transitions can help you keep your reader rolling along smoothly without sudden jumps from one topic to another.

***Combined with a good outline,
transitions can help ensure a smooth ride for your reader.***

"But *How* Do I Write an Essay?"

So far, we've been talking mainly about tools for getting your point across in essay writing, knowing that if you can write a good essay, you can more easily do other forms of nonfiction writing. But besides *intro, body, conclusion* (or *lead, story, close*), isn't there more information on *how* to write a good essay?

Yes, there is. It starts by learning a bit about different types of essays, because

not all essays have the same purpose.

It's like this: If you were learning to cook, you wouldn't learn how to steam rice and nothing else, would you? You would learn how to prepare meat so it's tender and juicy. You would learn how to cook vegetables so their natural flavors and nutrients weren't lost along the way. You would learn how to prepare pasta so it wasn't too mushy or too chewy.

And then you would learn how to put all these different skills together, eventually being able to create your own delicious and nutritious meals, depending on your purpose at the time.

Essay writing is similar.

If you learn how to do a few different kinds of essays well, you will then be able to use those skills to create any kind of essay you want, depending on your purpose at the time. And you will be confident you can always get your point across.

The purpose of the next few chapters is to teach you about four common essay types.

Learning these will help give you more ideas on *how* to organize your introductions, bodies and conclusions—and be sure you make your point each time.

The Narrative Essay

The first type of essay we'll go over is called *the narrative essay.*

A **narrative essay**

tells a story.

It comes from the word *narrate*, which means *to tell a story in speech or in writing.*

As defined earlier, by **story** is meant

the telling or description of something that happened, usually as a sequence of actions.

In a narrative essay, this happens, then that happens, then this happens, and so on. Normally, it is told from a particular viewpoint, whether it's your own or someone else's.

When you want to tell about a series of events, it's probably a narrative essay.

Here's an example of the beginning of a narrative essay from the writer's viewpoint:

> The first thing I checked was to see if I had broken any bones. Arms, hands, feet, legs, ribs—everything seemed okay. Just some bruises, and a broken bicycle helmet. But what happened over the next few hours changed my life forever.

Here's an example from someone else's viewpoint:

> One day Sergio decided, "I'm going to get rich. Really rich!" The very next day he started. He worked out all his plans, got all his materials together, decided on how to promote, set prices for his product and by that afternoon he was open for business. The sign said, "Lemonade 99 cents." It was a pretty good start—for an 8-year-old. Who knew where it would eventually lead?

In both these examples, a lead is used to get the reader interested, to lead them in. For a narrative essay, you usually aren't writing an intro that explains the purpose of the essay. You're leading the reader right into the story you want to tell.

Obviously, the outline for the body of a narrative essay will show the parts of the story you plan to tell.

The conclusion of a narrative essay is where you will most likely communicate your overall message. For the first example, we might imagine the overall message is going to be about how little things can have big effects. For the second one we can imagine the final point might be about how Sergio lived a life focused on making money until one day he decided that having lots of money wasn't all that important.

As a tip on narrative essays,

sometimes it's interesting to start at the end of the story,

then come back to the beginning and tell the events in the order that shows how that ending came about. Sometimes fiction books and movies do this for the same reason: it's a little different and can therefore be more interesting.

In the same way, you can start with your overall message instead of putting it at the end. Or you can hint at your overall message at the beginning and then make it strongly at the end—whatever you think works best.

The skills you learn from narrative essays can be applied in many ways. Here are a few examples:

- Writing biographies and autobiographies.
- Preparing a legal case that wants to walk the judge or jury through a sequence of events.
- Writing up the history of a line of research, for example the steps that led to the discovery of a cure for a disease.
- Explaining in writing how something happened.

If you like telling a story, narrative essays should come naturally to you.

The Descriptive Essay

A **descriptive essay**

describes something well, such as a person, place or event.

Descriptive essays are particularly useful when the main purpose of the essay is to put the reader in someone else's shoes or in some particular place and time. By helping the reader "live" an experience, you can make your point in a more realistic way.

When doing a description of a person, you can give details on what they look like, describe their hopes and dreams, how they act, or how they interact with others. It can also focus on just one or two key characteristics of their personality: their enthusiasm, their humor, their stubbornness, their intelligence, their creativity, and so on. This type of descriptive essay is often called a *character sketch.* Character sketches can be a lot of fun, especially when the writer doesn't say who the character sketch is about, and the reader has to try to figure it out!

Whether you are describing a person, place or event, you want to make the reader feel like he or she is there, like they can feel the place, see the person, hear the sounds.

Here's an example of a paragraph that uses description to put the reader in the scene:

> The wave was as tall as a two-story building, and it was alive with terrifying force! It rolled violently toward the beach full of fans who just a second ago were cheering. Now they were silent. Tonya and her surfboard had disappeared under the curl. Seconds went by. The wave kept coming. Finally, she shot out of the shrinking tunnel just ahead of the crashing water. Everyone started screaming.

The key to a good descriptive essay:

Use details that paint a picture in the reader's mind.

In a descriptive essay, you might have a particular message or point you are trying to make, but that doesn't mean you have to state it exactly. Sometimes it works to make your description so good that the reader can tell what the point is just from reading the description.

Being able to write a good descriptive essay will help you learn to see the world through other people's eyes, a skill useful in many aspects of writing—and life!

The Expository Essay

An **expository essay**

gives information that explains or brings something into view.

The name comes from the word *expose,* which means to uncover something. An expository essay is often used when you have studied something or learned something, and you want to explain it to the reader.

Many essays for school are like this. For example, you study about some aspect of nutrition and then you need to write an essay about it. You're explaining what you learned through your essay.

Because of this, expository essays are the type that can most easily become boring, especially if you are basically summarizing something you just read about. Remember, summaries tend to be boring, details tend to be interesting.

Something to keep in mind in all writing is this:

***If you're not really that interested,
your reader won't be either.***

Therefore, in writing an expository essay, try to *expose* new knowledge or new opinions you have about the information to your reader. To repeat and highlight something said in chapter 3:

***Almost every teacher will tell you their favorite students are
the ones who are not afraid to say what they think,
as long as they say it well.***

When writing an expository essay, if you find you don't seem to have anything very interesting to say, you might want to ask yourself why. There's no way to get your point across in writing if you don't actually have a point to make!

It often means you should do more study, or study more deeply the topic you're trying to write an expository essay about.

Realize that professionals in virtually all fields are constantly discovering that they don't know enough to speak or write intelligently on a subject. What do they do? They do more study, or study more deeply the topic they are trying to communicate on.

You'll know when you are ready to write. It will be when you know you have something to say.

As for organizing an expository essay, you will usually build your outline on the various facts or ideas that led to your conclusion.

For examples of good expository writing, read good reporting. This will more often be found in magazines than in newspapers. Magazines come out less often so the reporters who are writing the articles have more time to really dig into the topic, expose the information they are looking for, then put together a good article.

If you like getting to the bottom of things and then telling people about it, expository essays are for you!

The Persuasive Essay

The last type of essay we will cover is the **persuasive essay**, which tries to persuade or convince someone of something.

Of the four types of essays discussed here, the persuasive essay most demands that the writer have a viewpoint, conclusion or opinion. There has to be *something* you are trying to convince or persuade the reader of.

For this reason, essay assignments that ask for opinions or conclusions are usually the most interesting for both the writer and the reader. Unfortunately, students are often only asked for expository writing, which doesn't necessarily demand that students share their own views, opinions or ideas—though you still can!

When writing a persuasive essay, realize that you don't have to prefer the side of an argument you are making. Students who study debate often practice arguing the opposite side to the one they believe in. But you need to take a stance. You need to represent a particular view in order to persuade or convince someone of something.

Persuasive essays are the type where you will often want to present counter-arguments, as discussed in chapter 10.

If you are writing a persuasive essay because you've been asked for *your* views, be glad. Why?

What you think is more interesting than what the book said.

—especially to a teacher who may have read the same essay over and over for years!

As your responsibilities grow in life, you will probably discover that your ability to develop and create a good persuasive essay will prove invaluable in ways you never imagined!

Outside the Box

As you gain experience, you will probably find times when the essay you are writing doesn't seem to fit neatly into one of the types described in the previous chapters.

For example, you might write a *narrative* essay that has detailed *descriptions* in it. Or you might write an *expository* essay that has an important opinion you want to *persuade* your reader to agree with.

This is not something to be concerned about. It's to be expected. You are gaining skills so you can *use* them in your writing to get your point across.

The purpose of describing these four types of essays is to help you understand essay writing better, to help you become a better writer, not to limit you.

Plus, just because a narrative essay has descriptions in it doesn't mean it's not a narrative essay. Just because an expository essay has persuasion in it, doesn't mean it's not an expository essay.

Unless you are specifically asked for, or practicing, a particular type of essay, it doesn't matter in the end what kind of essay it is. What matters is that you know what you want to say, and you successfully say it!

The key is this: By first learning how to write these different kinds of essays well, you will gain essay-writing skills you can use in all your nonfiction writing. And if you write fiction, you'll be able to use the skills there as well!

In essay writing, don't be afraid to think outside the box—to do something different, unusual or creative.

As long you succeed in getting your point across, you can do whatever you want!

Getting It Right

Some essays are easy to write. What you need to cover is simple, you know what you want to say, and you know it can be done in two or three simple paragraphs.

Getting your point across isn't hard.

Some essays are more challenging because there's more to cover. You need to spend some time developing your ideas. You need to decide what type of essay it will be, and plan how to best organize it, including the intro and conclusion. Then there's *writing* the essay!

Getting your point across in a more challenging essay can involve quite a bit of work.

But there's more, because all we've covered so far is creating a draft, not a finished essay. What does that mean?

A **draft** is

> a version of a piece of writing
> not yet finalized.

There are almost no professions where the product comes out just right the first time. Even the best professionals need to review and improve what they've done to ensure it meets a certain standard of quality. Here are just a few examples:

- Stage actors (and all the stage managers, lights people, sound people and more) rehearse and rehearse and rehearse, and then do a dress rehearsal before the actual show is given to audiences.
- New machines have to go through testing, testing and more testing to ensure they actually work right before they are put out for sale.

- Trial lawyers who have fully prepared a case will still review all the facts and documents, the details around every witness, what they think the other side is going to present, and the details of their presentation before the trial ever starts.
- Professional athletic teams practice offensive and defensive plays and formations before they bring them to actual games.
- Even a good barber or hair stylist asks you how the haircut looks and makes any final adjustments before sending you out of the barbershop or salon!

All this is to say that very few writers are able to say exactly what they want to say the first time they write it down—even the very best, most experienced writers. Once they have a draft, they go through a process normally called *revising and rewriting.*

And that's before it ever gets to editors who are paid good money to help the writer ensure the written communication is the best it can be!

You're probably not being paid for the essays you are writing at this point, so it's not exactly the same. But you are trying to make sure your point gets across and that will always require at least some level of proofreading at least, and often some level of revising and rewriting as well.

Because young writers often confuse *revising and rewriting* with *proofreading,* let's start by defining these terms.

To **revise** (**and rewrite**) a piece of writing is

to review and make changes.

This can include changing certain words, reorganizing sentences or paragraphs, cutting small or large parts out, adding detail or explanations to parts that weren't clear, rewriting small or large portions, or (hopefully, not often) throwing the whole thing out and starting over.

It's all about getting the piece of writing to *work* right, getting it to make sense, getting it to say what you want it to say.

Proofreading is

finding and marking errors in a piece of writing
so it can be made error-free and ready for publishing.

Proofreading is always the final step before something is published. If very many errors are found, the writing might need to be proofread again to be sure errors weren't missed or new errors made while correcting it.[3]

Revising and rewriting is not really about looking for misspelled words, punctuation errors or grammar mistakes. That's proofreading.

After you have created a draft of your essay, you then review it to see if it works, if it makes sense, if it is coming together right, if it sounds good, looks good, and is logical from beginning to end.

And most importantly, *does it effectively get your point across?*

When you are done with revising and rewriting, you proofread it once or twice to pick up any small mistakes that you didn't notice while writing or revising the essay. Proofreading before revising can end up being wasted time, particularly when you end up making major changes and have to proofread it all over again.

Sometimes you will have a first draft, a second draft, even a third draft before you are sure you are ready to proofread and finalize an essay. It depends on what standard you are trying to achieve, how long and complex the essay is, how well you planned it beforehand, and how good you are at getting things right (or close to right) the first time in your writing.

3 It might be of some interest why it is called *proofreading.* Before computers and modern printers and copiers, written works like books and newspapers were prepared for printing by putting every single letter in place in a block, covering all the letters with ink, and then pressing paper to it—for every page. The first print of something was called a *proof.* The word *proof* is still used today to mean the first print of something which is then reviewed to make sure the printed version looks the way it is supposed to—a printed art piece, photograph, magazine or book rarely looks the same as it looked on a computer screen. So, *proofreading* is just that: *reading the proof.*

If you find yourself doing too many drafts, it might be a sign of one of these problems:

- You are not planning well enough before starting the writing.
- You don't yet understand the topic well enough to write something you like.
- You're losing the ability to see your writing freshly, as if you'd never seen it before.

On this last point, it's important to remember:

You already know what you wanted to say.
The reader doesn't.

When you "be" the reader, you see what the reader sees. Sometimes what you think it says on the page includes thoughts that you never actually got on the page.

There are a few tips that can help you see the writing newly:

1. You can set an important essay aside for a bit and put your attention on something else. When you come back to it, it's easier to have a "fresh" viewpoint, as if you hadn't seen it before.
2. Assuming you're working digitally, it can help to print it out and then read it newly. Sometimes this helps you see things you weren't seeing on the screen.
3. You can also try reading it aloud—or reading it aloud "in your head." By reading it aloud carefully, you can often see more clearly what you actually wrote, not what you *think* you wrote.

These tips can be used for both *revising and rewriting* as well as *proofreading.*

Good writers (and artists, musicians, actors and many other professionals) are good partly because they can assume the viewpoint of the reader (viewer, audience) very well. With practice, you can get good at it too.

Again, some essays are simple. You might be able to get them right on the first draft, even with no errors! Great. But longer, more complex essays will almost always require more work—more idea development, better planning (outlining), and two or three (or more) drafts to get it right.

And then, after all that, you need to do a good job of proofreading, because

the worst thing that can happen to a great essay is to have the communication destroyed by silly mistakes!

Once you understand the difference between *revising and rewriting* and *proofreading*, and you are skilled at both, you are well on your way to getting your point across every time.

Feedback

Feedback is

comments, usually helpful, about
how well someone is doing something.

An important part of developing a work of art, a product or a service is getting useful feedback. This can apply to writing as well.

For professional writers, sometimes editors provide this. But most writers get feedback from whomever they choose before their book or article gets to an editor.

For students, this can be a problem because instructors usually don't want students helping other students with their work. This means the instructor is the one providing the feedback, and that's normally a good thing. It's part of the instructor's job to help students learn to write, and he or she will usually be good at doing it. So, the feedback should be good feedback.

Still, getting feedback from an instructor is not the same as getting it from a fellow student.

In the working world, employees expect feedback on how well they are doing from their boss. But often, when they are developing some product or skill, they prefer to get feedback from their peers first.

A **peer** is

someone who is the same age
or at the same level or position.

For many people, it's easier to get feedback from peers. They just feel more comfortable. People like this would rather have their friend tell them an essay is terrible than their instructor.

If you are writing essays for a class of any kind, the thing to do is find out from the instructor if student feedback is allowed. That way you'll know what your options are, and you won't find yourself doing something the instructor wouldn't approve of.

Some instructors may say it's fine to get feedback from peers and may encourage it. They will probably ask that you ensure it is only feedback and that you aren't having all or parts of your essay written or rewritten for you by someone else.

If feedback is allowed, you can have someone read a draft you've been working on and then ask question like these:

- "Did you get lost anywhere in the essay? If so, where?"
- "Was any part of the essay confusing?"
- "Did you get the overall message or point I was trying to make? If so, what do you think it was?"
- "Do you feel I said too much or said too little?"
- "Were there any parts you particularly liked?"

Asking questions like these keeps the writing in your hands where it belongs—whatever feedback they give, it's still your ideas, your words, your essay.

Getting feedback is often a normal part of the writing process. It's just that

when you are a student, you need to be very clear with your instructor on what feedback is allowed.

If peer feedback isn't allowed by a particular instructor or for a particular course or class, don't let that be an excuse for lower quality writing. Use it as an opportunity to see how well you can assume the reader's viewpoint and get your point across without any feedback—except the instructor's.

If you apply everything you're learning in this book, it's almost guaranteed the instructor's feedback will be very positive!

"Whose Ideas Are These?"

Let's take a moment and return to the definition of essay:

a short piece of writing on some subject,
usually presenting the writer's personal views

Let's focus on those last few words: *the writer's personal views.*

A common mistake for young essay writers is to think their own ideas aren't interesting enough to write about, so they just write using other people's ideas. It's true that an essay can include mention of other people's ideas, but the essay should focus on what *the writer* has to say.

When you want to use someone else's ideas in an essay, the key is to make it clear to the reader that you are doing so. Otherwise, you are plagiarizing.

To **plagiarize** is

to use someone else's words or ideas in writing
without clearly saying you are doing so.

Pretending someone else's ideas are yours is actually a form of stealing.

Finding a mountain bike that's not yours and keeping it is stealing. If you're a minor, you can find yourself in juvenile court. If you're an adult, you can be sent to jail.

Finding some written material, copying and pasting it into an essay you're writing, changing a few things, and turning it in as your own ideas is stealing. A junior high or high school student *might not* get kicked out of school for plagiarizing—the first time. A college student might. A working professional can be fired, sued, or just publicly embarrassed and never trusted again.

You can say, "Oh, I didn't know what I did was plagiarism." But that doesn't really matter. Part of the purpose of this chapter is to make sure you do know.

Unfortunately, in some places and in some schools, "helping" other students by writing essays or doing other work for them is considered acceptable by students (and sometimes even by their parents). If your purpose is to learn, there's nothing ethical about presenting someone else's work as your own. It's simply dishonest.

Students who go through high school this way are probably the ones who go online to buy essays for college admissions or for college classes. It's true. It happens. Imagine buying a painting and having it shipped to you, then putting your name on it and showing it to your art teacher, saying, "Look how well you've taught me!" Ouch.

Fortunately, avoiding plagiarism is easy: whenever you use someone else's words or ideas, tell the reader whose ideas or words they are and where you got them.

This mostly comes up when doing expository writing, such as a research paper—you've studied some topic and have a lot of information you want to present and an overall point or conclusion you want to make about it.

This really only becomes a problem when students don't understand the difference between ideas that are *common knowledge* and ideas that aren't.

So what is common knowledge?

Common knowledge is

information (usually facts, not opinion)
that you can find in many places;
information most people know.

If you wrote, "The population of India is over one billion," you would not need to say whose idea this was because anyone can find this information in many places. It is common knowledge, not one person's idea or one person's particular wording.

Here are more examples of common knowledge:

- The sun is 93 million miles away.
- New York City is home to more professional sports teams than any other city.
- Some people do not believe climate change is being caused by humans.
- A narrative essay is an essay that tells a story.
- Charles Dickens was a very successful author.
- Apple sells computers, phones, smart watches and tablets.

Here are examples of things most people would not consider common knowledge, with examples of different ways to show where the information can be found:

> The closest sun outside our solar system is Alpha Centauri, which is actually a group of three suns about 25 trillion miles away from us. ("Alpha Centauri: Nearest Star System to Earth," space.com)
>
> There are many reasons why New Yorkers think they have the best sports town in America. To me, the funniest one comes from a 2013 article in USA Today by Nick Schwartz entitled "20 Reasons Why New York Is the Best Sports City in the World." Number 16 on the list is "Nathan's hot dog eating contest." I think calling hot dog eating a sport is hilarious!
>
> Yes, the climate is changing, but according to Tonya T. Neaves, Director, Centers on the Public Service at George Mason University: "Natural forces beyond human control are also gradually affecting our climate." (nbcnews.com)

According to the book *Getting Your Point Across in Writing* (Heron Books, 2019): "If you like telling a story, narrative essays should come naturally to you." Unfortunately, I didn't find this to be true for me.

Charles Dickens was not only a successful author, when he wrote the book *David Copperfield,* he apparently did something nobody had ever done before by writing a novel that "simply followed a character through his everyday life."[1]

For this last example, at the bottom of the page is this:

1: biography.com/people/charles-dickens-9274087

As you can see, there are different ways you can show where the information came from. What's important is to

provide enough information so that the reader can find the source of the information easily.

You don't want to ever mislead the reader about which ideas belong to whom in any writing you've done.

And if you're ever asked the question "Whose ideas are these anyway?" you should always be able to answer honestly, "Unless otherwise stated, they're all mine."

Putting It All Together

To get your point across in writing, the following step-by-step guide can be used in combination with the short checklist that follows on the next page.

Try them out and see how they work for you. And don't be surprised if you soon find yourself consistently writing essays that have impact!

Essay Writing Guide

1. If you're answering a question, make sure you understand it.
2. Develop your ideas.
3. Work out your point.
4. Decide what type of essay will work best.
5. Create an outline.
6. Write a draft, polishing the lead and close last.
7. Set it aside, if possible.
8. "Be" the reader and read it freshly.
9. Note what's working and what's not.
10. Revise and rewrite it.
11. Proofread it.
12. If allowed, get feedback.
13. Revise, rewrite and re-proofread as needed.
14. Get it read!

Essay Writing Checklist

- ☐ Does the style or type of essay fit the purpose?
- ☐ Does it have a clear message that is *yours*?
- ☐ Does it have enough details for interest and support of the message?
- ☐ Does it start off well?
- ☐ Does it flow logically and have smooth transitions?
- ☐ Does it end smoothly?
- ☐ Are other people's ideas correctly identified?
- ☐ Is it free of silly mistakes?
- ☐ Does it get your point across?
- ☐ Are you happy with it?

Final Tips
(for aspiring professionals)

From intros to conclusions, from supporting details to outlines, this book has covered a lot of information and advice on how to get your point across in writing.

But for you, someone aspiring to be more than just a good writer—maybe even a great one—the best advice has been saved for last. It's a short list.

1. Keep reading.

Read great writing. It can be found everywhere. Classic literature. Modern books. Many magazines employ very talented writers no matter what subject you're interested in. Great writing is all around you, but you have to put your hands on it and *read* it.

And read a lot of it aloud. The language has a feel and sound. Reading aloud brings that out. So does listening to it, and you can find great writing not only in audio books but in recorded speeches.

Your most important training in becoming a great writer is to read as much great writing as you can get your hands on.

2. Keep writing.

Nothing could be more obvious.

And even if you only want to write fiction or poetry and never intend on writing nonfiction professionally, you will need to use your nonfiction writing skills at some point. Plus it never hurts to practice as many different kinds of writing as you can.

Whatever else you do, keep writing. And writing and writing.

3. Don't be afraid to borrow ideas.

We are all learning from each other all the time. Take something you read that you liked and try to imitate the style in your own writing. And do it again and again.

Don't worry about "your own style." It will come—after many thousands and thousands of written words.

4. Take chances.

Experiment. Try something totally new. Be creative. Take chances.

Every great artist broke rules.

A Note on This Fifth Edition

The previous edition of *Getting Your Point Across in Writing* included an appendix of sample essays. This edition does not. They were removed for the following reasons:

1. For some student writers, the shorter samples came across as overly simplistic and therefore not useful. For others, the more sophisticated samples left them feeling inadequate. Finding a happy medium where samples served all young writers proved problematic.

2. Though sample sentences and paragraphs *are* provided throughout the book to illustrate individual points of essay writing, the editors felt the provision of full essays tended to *give too much.* Challenging young writers to come up with their own full essays was considered important in fostering creativity.

3. Finally, and most importantly, whereas sample essays created specifically for instructional purposes often feel contrived, real essays for real readers are all around us. The editors felt it was this real world of essay writing that should be modeled, whether the essays are found in news media, magazines, blogs or books.

Teachers can, of course, find and collect sample essays that best suit their students of different abilities—and we expect they will. Better yet, they can help students discover the world of nonfiction writing that surrounds them and encourage students to share what they find. In this way, students can model the essay writers who have most impacted them personally.

Such an approach seemed more consistent with this latest edition of *Getting Your Point Across in Writing,* which was specifically designed to emphasize function over form and the use of basic tools by young writers learning *how to write essays that have impact!*

Editors

Materials List

GETTING YOUR POINT ACROSS IN WRITING

HOW TO WRITE ESSAYS THAT HAVE IMPACT

Book

Getting Your Point Across in Writing, How to Write Essays That Have Impact, Heron Books

Other Materials

None

10 April 2019

Materials List

GETTING YOUR POINT ACROSS IN WRITING
HOW TO WRITE ESSAYS THAT HAVE IMPACT

Book

Getting Your Point Across in Writing, How to Write Essays That Have Impact, Heron Books

Other Materials

None

10 April 2019

SUBSCRIBER SCHOOLS

Delphian School
K-12 boarding and day
20950 SW Rock Creek Rd
Sheridan, OR 97378
503.843.3521
delphian.org

Delphi Academy of Boston
PreK-8 day
564 Blue Hill Ave
Milton, MA 02186
617.333.9610
delphiboston.org

Delphi Academy of Los Angeles
PreK-12 day
11341 Brainard Ave
Lake View Terrace, CA 91342
818.583.1070
delphila.org

Oak Crest Private School
PreK-8 day
1200 E Jackson Rd, Bldg 2
Carrollton, Texas 75006
214.483.5400
oakcrestschool.org

Delphi Academy of Florida
PreK-12 day
1831 Drew St
Clearwater, FL 33765
727.447.6385
delphifl.org

Ability School
PreK-8 day
75 Knickerbocker Rd
Englewood, NJ 07631
201.871.8808
abilityschoolnj.com

Whether kindergarten through 3rd, 6th, 8th or 12th grade, subscriber schools license with Heron Books to use the DELPHI PROGRAM™ which includes a comprehensive curriculum and structure designed to encourage every student to reason, to think creatively, to look at the world independently, and to evaluate information for its relative importance and usefulness. To see the Delphi Program in action, visit any of the above subscriber schools. For information on subscriber school services and materials, email info@heronbooks.com.

Lightning Source UK Ltd.
Milton Keynes UK
UKHW050936210622
404711UK00003B/92

9 780897 391436